Grammaropolis
PRESENTS

Meet the

Parts of Speech

8
POPULATION

Student Workbook

THIRD GRADE

written by

THE MAYOR OF GRAMMAROPOLIS

HOUSTON

Edited by Christopher Knight
Cover and Interior Design by Mckee Frazior
Character Design by Powerhouse Animation

ISBN: 9781644420324
Copyright © 2020 by Grammaropolis LLC
Illustrations copyright © 2020 by Grammaropolis LLC
All rights reserved.
Published by Grammaropolis
Distributed by Six Foot Press
Printed in the U.S.A.

Grammaropolis.com
Six Foot Press.com

Table of Contents

From the Desk of the Mayor   5

Meet the Parts of Speech!   6

Meet the Nouns!   7
· Common Nouns and Proper Nouns   8
· Concrete Nouns and Abstract Nouns   9
· Collective Nouns   10
· Compound Nouns   11
· Singular Nouns and Plural Nouns   12
· Writing with Nouns   13
· Assessment – The Big Noun Quiz!   14

Meet the Verbs!   15
· Action Verbs Express Action   16
· Transitive Action Verbs   17
· Intransitive Action Verbs   18
· Linking Verbs Express a State of Being   19
· Action Verb or Linking Verb?   20
· Irregular Past Tense Verbs   21
· Writing with Verbs   22
· Assessment – The Big Verb Quiz!   23

Meet the Adjectives!   24
· Identifying Adjectives   25
· Words Adjectives Modify   26
· Demonstrative, Possessive, and Interrogative Adjectives   27
· Comparative and Superlative Adjectives   28
· Writing with Adjectives   29
· Assessment - The Big Adjective Quiz!   30

Meet the Adverbs!   31
· Identifying Adverbs   32
· Adverbs Can Tell "Where," "When," or "How"   33
· Words Adverbs Modify   34
· Comparative and Superlative Adverbs   35
· Writing with Adverbs   36
· Assessment – The Big Adverb Quiz!   37

Table of Contents

Meet the Pronouns! 38
- Why We Use Pronouns 39
- Pronouns and Antecedents 40
- Subjective and Objective Pronouns 41
- Intensive and Reflexive Pronouns 42
- Pronoun or Adjective? 43
- Writing with Pronouns 44
- Assessment – The Big Pronoun Quiz! 45

Meet the Conjunctions! 46
- Coordinating Conjunctions 47
- Correlative Conjunctions 48
- Subordinating Conjunctions 49
- Identifying Conjunctions 50
- Writing with Conjunctions 51
- Assessment – The Big Conjunction Quiz! 52

Meet the Prepositions! 53
- Identifying Prepositions 54
- Prepositional Phrases 55
- Preposition or Adverb? 56
- Writing with Prepositions 57
- Assessment – The Big Preposition Quiz! 58

Meet the Interjections! 59
- Identifying Interjections 60
- Writing with Interjections 61
- Assessment – The Big Interjection Quiz! 62

The Big Quiz Answer Key! 63

For information on how Grammaropolis correlates to state standards,
please visit us online at edu.grammaropolis.com.

FROM THE DESK OF THE MAYOR

There's a reason students can instantly recall everything that happened in their favorite movies but struggle to retain much of the important information you're trying to cover in school: people are hard-wired to remember what we connect with on an emotional level.

That's why grammar is so hard to teach. (As a former grammar teacher myself, I know firsthand.) Traditional materials are dry, abstract, and lifeless. There's nothing to connect with. Put simply, grammar is boring.

But it doesn't have to be! Our story-based approach combines traditional instruction with original narrative content, appealing to different learning styles and encouraging students to make a deeper connection with the elements of grammar.

In Grammaropolis, adverbs don't just modify verbs; adverbs are bossy! They tell the verbs **where** to go, **when** to leave, and **how** to get there. A pronoun doesn't just replace a noun; Roger the pronoun is a shady character who's always trying to trick Nelson the noun into giving up his spot.

And it works! Our mobile apps have already been downloaded over 2.5 million times, and thousands of schools and districts use our web-based site license. In other words, we don't skimp on the vegetables; we just make them taste good.

Thanks so much for visiting Grammaropolis. I hope you enjoy your stay!

— *The Mayor*

Meet the Parts of Speech!

Nouns

name a person, place, thing, or idea.

Verbs

express action or a state of being.

Adverbs

modify a verb, an adjective, or another adverb.

Adjectives

modify a noun or pronoun.

Prepositions

show a logical relationship or locate an object in time or space.

Pronouns

take the place of one or more nouns or pronouns.

Interjections

express strong or mild emotion.

Conjunctions

join words or word groups.

Grammaropolis

Meet the Nouns!

EXAMPLES

PERSON: <u>Clarence</u> listened intently to his baseball <u>coach</u>.

PLACE: Jeannie gave a great presentation on <u>Tanzania</u>.

THING: Mila put <u>sugar</u> and <u>cinnamon</u> on her <u>toast</u>.

IDEA: Eva felt a terrible <u>sadness</u> when her sister left.

Common Nouns and Proper Nouns

Mrs. Ennis is my favorite **teacher**.
Her new **car** is a Subaru.

Mrs. Ennis is my favorite teacher.
Her new car is a Subaru.

Pro Tip:
A noun that names a general person, place, thing, or idea is called a **common noun**.

Pro Tip:
A noun that names a specific person, place, thing, or idea is called a **proper noun**.

Let's Practice!

Instructions:
In each of the following sentences, circle any common nouns and underline any proper nouns.

EXAMPLE:
My little brother Jerry likes to eat Twinkies in the park.

1. Kevin never goes straight home after school.

2. Instead, he runs across the street to the library.

3. Once he gets to the library, Kevin and his friend Gbemi read books about monsters.

4. Their favorite monster is Frankenstein, but they like Dracula, too.

5. Gbemi once scared Kevin so much that he ran out of the room squealing.

Your turn!

Instructions:
Write a sentence that includes at least one proper noun, a sentence that includes at least one common noun, and a sentence that includes at least one of each. Circle the common nouns and underline the proper nouns.

1. proper _____

2. common _____

3. one of each _____

Concrete Nouns and Abstract Nouns

I bought a toy __car__ with my very own __money__.

Kevin's new toy car brought him __joy__ and __elation__.

FIVE SENSES

Pro Tip:
A **concrete noun** names a person, place, or thing that can be perceived by one or more of the five senses.

Pro Tip:
An **abstract noun** names an idea or quality that cannot be perceived by any of the five senses.

Let's Practice!

Instructions:
In each of the following sentences, circle any concrete nouns and underline any abstract nouns.

EXAMPLE:

Whenever happiness fills Jackie's heart, she bakes her little brother a cake.

1. Some people express confusion when you ask them to pat their own shoulders.

2. Eating great pancakes is one of life's simple pleasures.

3. I go to the mountains with the goal of enjoying the solitude.

4. As Jaxon got older, he focused more on personal growth and less on personal riches.

5. Your cookies are as delicious as Lyall's pudding.

Your turn!

Instructions:
Write a sentence that includes at least one concrete noun, a sentence that includes at least one abstract noun, and a sentence that includes at least one of each. Circle the concrete nouns and underline the abstract nouns.

1. concrete _____

2. abstract _____

3. one of each _____

Collective Nouns

I accidentally dropped my shoe, and it bounced down the entire **flight** of stairs.

Sometimes I wonder if it's possible to count all of the stars in the **galaxy**.

Pro Tip:
A **collective noun** is a singular noun that names a group.

Let's practice!

Instructions:
Circle all of the collective nouns in the each of the following sentences.

EXAMPLE:
Our picnic was cut short by a (swarm) of angry bees.

1. Would someone please shuffle this deck of cards before we play?

2. Judith's favorite thing about archery was carrying a quiver of arrows on her back.

3. Lola really had to practice her songs before she auditioned for the choir.

4. A standard ream of paper contains five hundred sheets.

5. Rex had to water all of the peach trees in the orchard before he went to school.

Your turn!

Instructions:
Use the collective nouns below to write your very own sentences.

1. pack _____

2. fleet _____

3. bouquet _____

Compound Nouns

Pro Tip:
*A **compound noun** is formed when two or more words combine to make a single noun. A compound noun can be one single word, two words, or words connected by hyphens.*

Let's practice!

Instructions:
Circle all of the compound nouns in each of the following sentences.

EXAMPLE:
The girls and boys played football in the backyard.

1. All Kelli wanted for her birthday was a big milkshake.

2. I'm pretty sure we're going to be able to build a snowman today.

3. Molly's stepbrother is a lot nicer than her brother-in-law.

4. Mr. Cullinan had to remind me that it's not polite to wear headphones in class.

5. Owen forgot to wash his hands, so he left fingerprints all over the new window.

Your turn!

Instructions:
Create your own compound nouns by adding another word to the words below.

dog	_____	box	_____
chair	_____	water	_____
show	_____	sun	_____
pine	_____	head	_____

Singular Nouns and Plural Nouns

Singular Nouns:
That <u>child</u> over there caught an enormous <u>trout</u>.

Plural Nouns:
How can those <u>children</u> over there be catching so many <u>trout</u>?

Pro Tip:
A **singular noun** names a single person, place, thing, or idea. A **plural noun** names more than one person, place, thing, or idea.

Pro Tip:
Most nouns are made plural by adding -s, or -es to the singular form. The ones that don't are called **irregular** plural nouns.

Let's Practice!

Instructions:
In each of the following sentences, circle any singular nouns and underline any plural nouns.

EXAMPLE:

The most important item on your grocery list is a big bag of mangoes.

1. Please put the books on those shelves across the hall.

2. I asked Jake if he wanted one potato or two potatoes.

3. The movie is about three thieves who store their stolen loot in dormant volcanoes.

4. Clarissa's worst day ever involved an unfortunate encounter with cacti.

5. Sheep don't tend to get along with even one ox, let alone multiple oxen.

Your turn!

Instructions:
Turn the following singular nouns into plural nouns. Remember that some might be irregular!

loaf _____   pear _____

foot _____   joke _____

smile _____   tax _____

mouse _____   goose _____

Writing with Nouns

INSTRUCTIONS (PART ONE):
Brainstorm some of your favorite nouns for each of the following categories.

PROPER	CONCRETE	ABSTRACT	COLLECTIVE	COMPOUND
-----------------	-----------------	-----------------	-----------------	-----------------
-----------------	-----------------	-----------------	-----------------	-----------------
-----------------	-----------------	-----------------	-----------------	-----------------
-----------------	-----------------	-----------------	-----------------	-----------------

INSTRUCTIONS (PART TWO):
Now choose TWO nouns from each of your categories and use them to write a short story. Don't forget to circle the nouns when you use them!

_____

_____

_____

_____

_____

_____

_____

Grammaropolis

The Big Noun Quiz!

INSTRUCTIONS: Classify the noun type for the <u>underlined nouns</u> below from among the available options.

1. A <u>crew</u> of volunteers keeps litter out of the city's riverbed.
   ○ abstract   ○ collective   ○ proper   ○ compound

2. Birds sometimes nest right at the top of the <u>streetlamp</u> on the corner.
   ○ abstract   ○ collective   ○ proper   ○ compound

3. If you can live with honor and <u>integrity</u>, you will go far.
   ○ abstract   ○ collective   ○ proper   ○ compound

4. Zadie's class had a wonderful time visiting <u>Houston</u>.
   ○ abstract   ○ collective   ○ proper   ○ compound

5. Did you know that a group of crows is called a <u>murder</u> of crows?
   ○ abstract   ○ collective   ○ proper   ○ compound

INSTRUCTIONS: Indicate whether the <u>underlined nouns</u> below are singular or plural nouns.

6. Jason's <u>feet</u> are enormous!
   ○ singular   ○ plural

7. I want to hear tales of <u>strength</u> and courage.
   ○ singular   ○ plural

8. A <u>host</u> of reporters showed up in anticipation of the big announcement.
   ○ singular   ○ plural

9. New Mexico is home to some of the nicest <u>men</u> and women I know.
   ○ singular   ○ plural

10. Students and teachers gathered by the <u>grove</u> of pine trees for a big science lesson.
    ○ singular   ○ plural

Grammaropolis

Meet the Verbs!

I am an action verb!

I express action.

EXAMPLES

The kids **<u>ride</u>** the bus.
Sarah **<u>invited</u>** me to the party.
T.J. **<u>will jump</u>** on his bed.

I am a linking verb.

I express a state of being.

EXAMPLES

Those muffins **<u>smell</u>** delicious.
Your play **<u>was</u>** enjoyable.
Annie's dad **<u>will be</u>** retired soon.

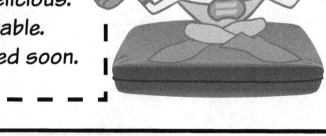

Action Verbs Express Action

Physical Action:
Marcus **painted** a lovely picture!

Mental Action:
I **prefer** chocolate to strawberry!

Pro Tip:
An action verb can express either **physical** action or **mental** action.

Let's practice!

Instructions:
Circle the action verb in each of the following sentences and indicate whether it is expressing physical or mental action.

EXAMPLE:

She (competed) in a gymnastics tournament this weekend.   ___physical action___

1.   Salvatore loved all of his birthday presents.   _____

2.   I will remember everything about this day.   _____

3.   Trevor wrote a wonderful book about chocolate cake.   _____

4.   Dr. Freeze saved my life with her superpowers.   _____

5.   Seventeen people came to my house last night.   _____

Your turn!

Instructions:
Write sentences using your own action verbs to express mental or physical action as indicated. Don't forget to circle the action verb you use!

1.   physical   _____

2.   mental   _____

3.   physical   _____

Grammaropolis

Transitive Action Verbs

Our teacher **gave** us a test.

Luckily, I **knew** the answers.

Pro Tip:
A *transitive action verb* passes its action on to the object of the verb.

Let's Practice!

Instructions:
Circle the transitive action verb in each sentence and draw an arrow to its object.

EXAMPLE:

I caught a bad cold, so I bought myself some tissues.

1. Sandra will make hamburgers for dinner tonight.

2. I memorized the answers to every question on the test.

3. Duncan builds sandcastles in his spare time.

4. Some people in my apartment building sing songs at night.

5. I will pour syrup all over my pancakes.

Your turn!

Instructions:
Write sentences with the verbs below as transitive action verbs. Don't forget to circle the verbs and draw arrows to their objects.

1. throw _____

2. save _____

3. burn _____

Intransitive Action Verbs

I _giggled_ and _snorted_ uncontrollably when my friend accidentally _sat_ on her lunch.

Pro Tip:
An **intransitive action verb** is an action verb that does not pass its action to an object.

Let's Practice!

Instructions:
Circle the intransitive action verb in each of the following sentences. (Don't circle any transitive action verbs!)

EXAMPLE:

When I make a mistake, I always (apologize).

1. Ferdinand and his wife lived in Malaysia for ten years.

2. Talia walked across the street from the salon to her favorite cafe.

3. I yelled loudly when the bell rang unexpectedly.

4. When your elders talk, you listen.

5. We launched a rocket into the air, and it flew incredibly high.

Your turn!

Instructions:
Write sentences using the verbs below as intransitive action verbs. Don't forget to circle the action verbs in the sentences!

1. sprint _____

2. cheer _____

3. end _____

Linking Verbs Express a State of Being

Linking verbs express a state of being. They "link" the subject to information that renames the subject.

"To be":
I **am** an astronaut.
She **was** outgoing.

Pro Tip:
Linking verbs often take a form of the verb "**to be**" but they don't have to!

Not "to be":
Bill **appears** exhausted.
That **smells** gross.

Let's practice!

Instructions:
Circle the linking verb in each of the following sentences.

EXAMPLE:

Jacob's brother (is) a fantastic artist.

1. You really seem pleased with yourself.

2. The big game will be so exciting!

3. Reginald and Rhonda sound super angry.

4. Dalton and his little brother, Kev, were so obnoxious last night after dessert.

5. Kylie's famous sugar cookies smelled absolutely spectacular.

Your turn!

Instructions:
Write three sentences using your own linking verbs. Make sure one of the sentences uses a linking verb that is not a form of "to be." Don't forget to circle the linking verbs!

1. _____

2. _____

3. _____

Grammaropolis

Action Verb or Linking Verb?

Linking Verb:
Your cooking **smelled** delicious!

Action Verb:
I **smelled** brownies in the oven the moment I walked inside.

Pro Tip:
Some words can be action verbs or linking verbs depending on how they're used.

Let's practice!

Instructions:
Circle the verb in each of the following sentences and indicate whether it is an action verb or a linking verb.

EXAMPLE:

Juliet always  calm in the face of danger.   linking verb

1. Valerie looked everywhere for her favorite stuffed animal.   _____

2. I grew more and more tired with every passing hour.   _____

3. Franklin remained in the car for at least thirty minutes.   _____

4. You look fantastic!   _____

5. Benji feels so happy every morning.   _____

Your turn!

Instructions:
Write sentences using the verbs below as action verbs or linking verbs as indicated. Don't forget to circle the verb in the sentence!

1. taste (action) _____

2. taste (linking) _____

3. grow (linking) _____

Irregular Past Tense Verbs

Bobby **took** his time eating dinner.

My sister **said** I could watch the movie with her.

Val couldn't believe that Annie **slept** until noon.

take → took

say → said

sleep → slept

Pro Tip:
An irregular past tense verb is a past tense verb that is not formed by putting -d or -ed after the present tense verb.

Let's practice!

Instructions:
Circle the correct form of the past tense verb in parentheses.

EXAMPLE:

I was so scared that I (ran, runned) straight to my room and slammed the door.

1. Lyall tossed me a newspaper, and I (caught, catched) it with my eyes closed.

2. Gerald (losed, lost) a bet with his best friend.

3. It took years, but they finally (found, finded) the buried treasure.

4. Nellie (freezed, froze) cubes of lemonade for some homemade popsicles.

5. To retire the last batter, Allison (threw, throwed) a perfect strike.

Your turn!

Instructions:
Write down the correct past tense verb form for each of the present tense verbs below.

build	_____	run	_____	come	_____
make	_____	throw	_____	speak	_____
hear	_____	find	_____	spend	_____

Grammaropolis

Writing with Verbs

INSTRUCTIONS (PART ONE):

Brainstorm some of your favorite action verbs and linking verbs. Make different lists for action verbs that express physical action and action verbs that express mental action.

PHYSICAL ACTION VERB	MENTAL ACTION VERB	LINKING VERB
-----------------------------	-----------------------------	-----------------------------
-----------------------------	-----------------------------	-----------------------------
-----------------------------	-----------------------------	-----------------------------
-----------------------------	-----------------------------	-----------------------------

INSTRUCTIONS (PART TWO):

Now choose TWO verbs from each of your categories and use them to write a short story. Don't forget to circle the verbs!

_____

_____

_____

_____

_____

_____

Grammaropolis

Name:

The Big Verb Quiz!

INSTRUCTIONS: Indicate whether the <u>underlined verb</u> below is an action verb or a linking verb.

1. No matter how difficult the situation becomes, Prax always <u>remains</u> calm.
    ○   action verb   ○   linking verb

2. Someone told me to <u>remain</u> where I was, but I didn't feel like staying put.
    ○   action verb   ○   linking verb

3. The baby koala slowly <u>tasted</u> the eucalyptus leaf with the tip of her tongue.
    ○   action verb   ○   linking verb

4. I <u>feel</u> awful after watching that movie about fast food.
    ○   action verb   ○   linking verb

5. If you water the seed enough, do you think that it <u>will grow</u> into a healthy plant?
    ○   action verb   ○   linking verb

INSTRUCTIONS: Indicate whether the <u>underlined action verb</u> below is transitive or intransitive.

6. Kevin <u>heard</u> the meteorologist's report and closed all the windows.
    ○   transitive   ○   intransitive

7. Nellie <u>sprinted</u> across the field as soon as the whistle blew.
    ○   transitive   ○   intransitive

8. The marathon is in only three days, and Bev <u>will run</u> it.
    ○   transitive   ○   intransitive

9. Sometimes I know the answer to her questions, and sometimes I <u>have</u> no idea.
    ○   transitive   ○   intransitive

10. Nyla's mom and dad <u>cooked</u> all night in preparation for her big party.
    ○   transitive   ○   intransitive

Meet the Adjectives!

EXAMPLES

WHAT KIND: Santiago picked out a <u>purple</u> necktie.

WHICH ONE: I want to open <u>that</u> package!

HOW MANY: It has been raining for <u>seven</u> days in a row.

HOW MUCH: Molly likes <u>more</u> salt than I do.

Identifying Adjectives

Kyle gave **his** **favorite** teacher an **enormous** **red** apple.

I'll give you **two** days to find **some** answers.

Pro Tip:
An adjective modifies one or more nouns or pronouns. It can tell **what kind, which one, how many** (a number or quantity) or **how much** (an amount).

Let's Practice!

Instructions:
Circle all the adjectives in the following sentences.

EXAMPLE:

(Those) (orange) flip-flops were given to me by (my) (best) and (oldest) friend.

1. New computers these days can be very expensive.

2. Winston accidentally poured hot coffee on his clean white pants.

3. Nobody was surprised when I opened the big window and yelled, "It's a beautiful day!"

4. Sara tried on three green dresses before deciding to buy the blue one.

5. Chase hid in the tiny, dark closet while we all looked for him.

Your turn!

Instructions:
Write sentences using more than one adjective in each sentence.
Don't forget to circle the adjectives!

1. _____

2. _____

3. _____

Words Adjectives Modify

Adjectives before:

The **brown** squirrel ran straight up the **tallest** tree in the park.

Adjectives after:

My teacher always looks **relieved** at the end of the week.

Pro Tip:
An adjective can come **before** or **after** the word or words it modifies.

Let's Practice!

Instructions:
Circle all of the adjectives in each of the following sentences.
Then draw an arrow from each adjective to the word it modifies.

EXAMPLE:

My sister was angry when I broke her favorite toy.

1. They say a sharp knife is safer to use than a dull knife.

2. We stayed at a remote cabin in the high mountains for a long time.

3. All students deserve a real opportunity to learn.

4. Her favorite t-shirt has purple and yellow stripes across the sleeves.

5. Even though the soup was hot and spicy, it was the best thing I'd ever tasted.

Your turn!

Instructions:
Write sentences using the adjectives below to describe a noun or pronoun. Circle each adjective and draw an arrow to the word it modifies.

1. zero _____

2. frozen _____

3. sweet _____

Grammaropolis

Demonstrative, Possessive, and Interrogative Adjectives

Demonstrative:
Please let me borrow **that** pen.

Possessive:
Sandra let me borrow **her** pen.

Interrogative:
Which pen belongs to Sandra?

Pro Tip:

A **demonstrative** adjective shows whether the noun it modifies is singular or plural and whether it is near or far.

A **possessive** adjective modifies a noun, showing possession or ownership.

An **interrogative** adjective is used to ask a question about a noun.

Let's Practice!

Instructions:
In each of the following sentences, draw an arrow from the <u>underlined adjective</u> to the word it modifies. Then indicate whether the adjective is demonstrative, possessive, or interrogative.

EXAMPLE:

<u>Those</u> blue shoes look amazing on you.   demonstrative

1. I really wish Mrs. Jansen would listen to <u>my</u> opinion.   _____

2. Niles wore <u>that</u> exact t-shirt to school yesterday.   _____

3. <u>Which</u> car is the one that broke the land speed record?   _____

4. Tasha and Bix always sell <u>their</u> famous pies on Tuesdays.   _____

5. <u>Whose</u> melted chocolate bar got all over Henry's coat?   _____

Your turn!

Instructions:
Write a sentence using the adjectives below as demonstrative (D), possessive (P), or interrogative (I). Circle the adjectives and draw arrows to the words they modify.

1. this (D)   _____

2. what (I)   _____

3. his (P)   _____

Grammaropolis

Comparative and Superlative Adjectives

Comparative:
I want a __smaller__ backpack than the one I have now.

Superlative:
My goal is to have the __smallest__ backpack in the world.

Pro Tip:
A **comparative adjective** is used to make a comparison between two nouns or pronouns.

Pro Tip:
A **superlative adjective** is used to describe the extreme quality of something and is used when talking about three or more nouns or pronouns.

Let's Practice!

Instructions:
In the sentences below, draw an arrow from the underlined adjective to the word it modifies. Then indicate whether the adjective is comparative or superlative.

EXAMPLE:

Umar drives the __fastest__ car in the whole class.   ___superlative___

1. Samantha is the __smartest__ person I have ever met.   _____

2. Is your hair __darker__ now than it was last year?   _____

3. Gerald's dog is the __meanest__ Labradoodle in the kennel.   _____

4. Pedro's new restaurant has the __fanciest__ appetizers in town.   _____

5. My kids are __louder__ than a freight train.   _____

Your turn!

Instructions:
Write sentences turning the adjectives below into comparative (C) or superlative (S) adjectives as indicated. Don't forget to circle the adjectives!

1. soft (S) _____

2. big (C) _____

3. slow (S) _____

4. tall (C) _____

Grammaropolis

Writing with Adjectives

INSTRUCTIONS (PART ONE):

Brainstorm a list of adjectives you might use to describe each of the nouns below.

1. homework	2. lunch	3. car	4. tree
- - - - - - - - - -	- - - - - - - - - -	- - - - - - - - - -	- - - - - - - - - -
- - - - - - - - - -	- - - - - - - - - -	- - - - - - - - - -	- - - - - - - - - -
- - - - - - - - - -	- - - - - - - - - -	- - - - - - - - - -	- - - - - - - - - -
- - - - - - - - - -	- - - - - - - - - -	- - - - - - - - - -	- - - - - - - - - -

INSTRUCTIONS (PART TWO):

Write a story that incorporates the nouns and adjectives above. Circle the adjectives when you use them!

_____

_____

_____

_____

_____

_____

The Big Adjective Quiz!

Name:

INSTRUCTIONS: Indicate whether the <u>underlined adjective</u> tells what kind, which one, how many, or how much.

1. That story had such a <u>sad</u> ending!
   ○ what kind   ○ which one   ○ how many   ○ how much

2. Dev's best friend never spends the night at <u>his</u> house for some reason.
   ○ what kind   ○ which one   ○ how many   ○ how much

3. We're all trying to use <u>less</u> water these days.
   ○ what kind   ○ which one   ○ how many   ○ how much

4. When I started training, I had no idea that a marathon was over <u>twenty</u> miles long.
   ○ what kind   ○ which one   ○ how many   ○ how much

5. Those <u>green</u> and yellow suspenders don't belong to me.
   ○ what kind   ○ which one   ○ how many   ○ how much

INSTRUCTIONS: Identify the word the <u>underlined adjective</u> modifies from among the available options.

6. That actress deserves <u>much</u> respect for how she played the role.
   ○ respect   ○ actress   ○ role   ○ she

7. The earth turns <u>maroon</u> after the rain because of all the iron in the soil.
   ○ rain   ○ earth   ○ soil   ○ iron

8. The <u>third</u> tent from the left is where you will find the acrobats.
   ○ left   ○ acrobats   ○ left   ○ tent

9. The winding path around my house can easily get covered by <u>overgrown</u> weeds.
   ○ path   ○ weeds   ○ house   ○ covered

10. <u>Most</u> people you talk to will say that vanilla pudding is quite tasty.
    ○ pudding   ○ vanilla   ○ you   ○ people

Grammaropolis

Meet the Adverbs!

EXAMPLES

MODIFYING A VERB: Come <u>here</u> and climb <u>carefully</u>.

MODIFYING AN ADJECTIVE: Why are you <u>never</u> happy?.

MODIFYING ANOTHER ADVERB: As soon as I heard the bell, I ran home <u>extremely</u> quickly.

Identifying Adverbs

Modifying Verbs:
Emily gazed **proudly** at her amazing work.

"proudly" modifies the verb "gazed" and tells how.

Modifying Adjectives:
Mom was **really** tired last night.

"really" modifies the adjective "tired" and tells to what extent (how much).

Modifying Other Adverbs:
Julian whispered **very** quietly.

"very" modifies the adverb "quietly" and tells to what extent (how much).

Pro Tip:
An **adverb** modifies a verb, adjective, or other adverb. It can tell more nouns or pronouns. It can tell **how, when, where** or to **what extent (how much).**

Let's Practice!

Instructions:
Circle all of the adverbs in the following sentences.

EXAMPLE:
I (never) listen to the advice of (very) loud people.

1. That beetle looked extremely afraid as it scampered unevenly across the ground.

2. Hummingbirds always fascinate me because they flap their wings so fast.

3. I ran home because I was very excited to read my new book immediately.

4. Mrs. Johnson is not pleased.

5. The bull aggressively charged at me, but I was safely protected behind a fence.

Your turn!

Instructions:
Write sentences of your own using adverbs to modify verbs, adjectives, or other adverbs. Don't forget to circle the adverbs you use!

1. _____

2. _____

3. _____

Adverbs Can Tell "Where," "When," or "How"

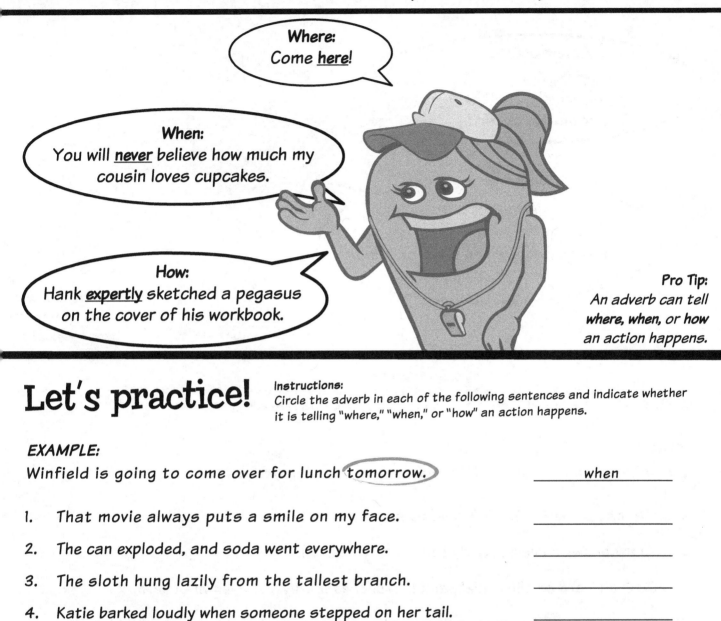

Where:
Come <u>here</u>!

When:
You will <u>never</u> believe how much my cousin loves cupcakes.

How:
Hank <u>expertly</u> sketched a pegasus on the cover of his workbook.

Pro Tip:
*An adverb can tell **where, when,** or **how** an action happens.*

Let's practice!

Instructions:
Circle the adverb in each of the following sentences and indicate whether it is telling "where," "when," or "how" an action happens.

EXAMPLE:
Winfield is going to come over for lunch tomorrow.   ____when____

1. That movie always puts a smile on my face.   _____

2. The can exploded, and soda went everywhere.   _____

3. The sloth hung lazily from the tallest branch.   _____

4. Katie barked loudly when someone stepped on her tail.   _____

5. You need to come up with a good answer soon.   _____

Your turn!

Instructions:
Write sentences below using adverbs to tell where, when, or how an action happens. Don't forget to circle the adverbs when you use them.

1. where   _____

2. when   _____

3. how   _____

Words Adverbs Modify

Adverb before:

Lynn <u>loudly</u> knocked on the front door until it opened.

Adverb after:

Lynn knocked <u>loudly</u> on the front door until it opened.

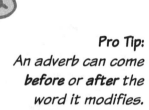

Pro Tip:
An adverb can come **before** or **after** the word it modifies.

Let's practice!

Instructions:
Circle all of the adverbs in each of the following sentences. Then draw an arrow from each adverb to the word it modifies.

EXAMPLE:
Jaxon (definitely) finished his homework, but he finished it (late.)

1. "Do not come here," I whispered angrily.

2. That sandwich unexpectedly tasted very delicious.

3. Benji bit hard on the radish, and it crunched loudly between his teeth.

4. I'm reading a really great book about bugs that thrive in extremely cold environments.

5. If you go there tomorrow, you will be very sorry.

Your turn!

Instructions:
Write sentences using the adverbs below. Circle each adverb and draw an arrow to the word it modifies.

1. totally _____

2. never _____

3. tomorrow _____

Grammaropolis

Comparative and Superlative Adverbs

Comparative:
I can dance **more obnoxiously** than you.
Betty threw the ball **farther** than I did.

Superlative:
I can dance the **most obnoxiously** of all.
Betty threw the ball the **farthest** of anyone on the whole team.

Pro Tip:
A **comparative adverb** is used when comparing two people, places or things.

Pro Tip:
A **superlative adverb** indicates the extreme quality of something. It is used when talking about three or more people, places or things.

Let's Practice!

Instructions:
In each of the following sentences, draw an arrow from underlined adverb to the word it modifies. Then indicate whether the adverb is comparative or superlative.

EXAMPLE:

I always run **faster** than I think is possible. _____comparative_____

1. I finished the race earlier than my nemesis. _____

2. That turtle hid the most quickly out of all of them. _____

3. Xavier jumped higher than Val did. _____

4. I usually work more quickly than you do. _____

5. Courtney's computer runs the most efficiently of all. _____

Your turn!

Instructions:
Write sentences turning the adverbs below into comparative (C) or superlative (S) adverbs as indicated. Don't forget to circle the adverb!

1. skillfully (S) _____

2. easily (C) _____

3. often (C) _____

4. softly (S) _____

Grammaropolis

Writing with Adverbs

INSTRUCTIONS (PART ONE):
Create adverbs that tell "how" by incorporating -ly to the end of the adjectives below.

ADJECTIVE	ADVERB
1. happy	1.
2. tight	2.
3. careful	3.
4. angry	4.
5. firm	5.

INSTRUCTIONS (PART TWO):
Fill in the blanks with your favorite adverbs that tell "where" and "when."

WHERE

1.

2.

WHEN

1.

2.

INSTRUCTIONS (PART THREE):
Write a story that incorporates all of the adverbs above. Circle the adverbs when you use them!

_____

_____

_____

_____

_____

_____

The Big Adverb Quiz!

INSTRUCTIONS: Identify the adverb in each of the sentences below from the available options.

1. Vikram often thinks about what's happening in other parts of the world.
   ○ thinks   ○ other   ○ often   ○ about

2. The cat's tail whipped fiercely back and forth as she eyed the bird.
   ○ whipped   ○ forth   ○ eyed   ○ tail

3. Sarah gazed wistfully at the tree swing and thought of her childhood.
   ○ wistfully   ○ swing   ○ gazed   ○ thought

4. When you make pasta, you should never put too much parsley on top.
   ○ should   ○ put   ○ never   ○ make

5. As soon as Hallie came home, she started writing in her journal.
   ○ came   ○ started   ○ as   ○ home

INSTRUCTIONS: Indicate whether the <u>underlined adverbs</u> below tell where, when, how, or to what extent.

6. Elizabeth <u>regularly</u> waters all the plants in her yard.
   ○ where   ○ when   ○ how

7. Yeah, yeah. I'll do my homework <u>tomorrow</u>.
   ○ where   ○ when   ○ how

8. "You'd better come <u>here</u> right now," Inez's mom said angrily.
   ○ where   ○ when   ○ how

9. I crept <u>quietly</u> across the carpet, but my sister still heard me.
   ○ where   ○ when   ○ how

10. Kallan <u>carelessly</u> scribbled some answers down right before the bell rang.
   ○ where   ○ when   ○ how

Grammaropolis

EXAMPLES

WITHOUT PRONOUNS: Jason and DeAndre ran a marathon in order to benefit their friends and neighbors.

WITH PRONOUNS: They ran it in order to benefit them.

Why We Use Pronouns

Without Pronouns:
Gavin is worried because Gavin sent Gavin a package, but Gavin still hasn't received the package.

With Pronouns:
Gavin is worried because <u>he</u> sent <u>himself</u> a package, but <u>he</u> still hasn't received <u>it</u>.

Pro Tip:
We use pronouns so that nouns or other pronouns in the sentence don't have to be repeated.

Let's practice!

Instructions:
Fill in the blanks in the sentences below using the pronouns that make sense.

EXAMPLE:

My cousin Jeremy is super nice. __*He*__ always gives me his old clothes.

1. Susan said that _____ wants me to go play in her yard tomorrow.

2. Liv looked at the box in her hands, put ____ down on the table, and walked away.

3. Win, Steve, and Ivor came to my house. _____ are all having a sleepover together!

4. Brea put so much salad on her plate that _____ had a hard time finishing ____ .

5. I was all alone, so I had to give _____ a haircut. _____ turned out great!

Your turn!

Instructions:
Write a short sentence using no pronouns. Then write the same sentence replacing the nouns with pronouns. Don't forget to circle the pronouns!

_____

_____

Pronouns and Antecedents

Pro Tip:
The word (or words) that the pronoun replaces is called the antecedent.

Let's practice!

Instructions:
Circle the pronoun in each of the following sentences and draw an arrow to the word it replaces.

EXAMPLE:
My sister loves cereal. She even eats it for lunch sometimes.

1. Michelle and Tonya bought themselves new t-shirts.

2. Molly dropped the glass, and it shattered all over the concrete.

3. Are these books for sale, or are they available for free?

4. Peter and I went to the store because we were out of food at home.

5. Can Shea stay longer? He is having so much fun!

Your turn!

Instructions:
Write sentences using the word pairs below as the pronoun and antecedent. Then circle the pronoun and draw an arrow to the antecedent.

1. Tim and I/we _____

2. table/it _____

3. Sharon/her _____

Grammaropolis

Subjective and Objective Pronouns

Subjective:
I enjoy movies.
She feels sick to her stomach.
You should be careful.

Objective:
Take me to a movie.
Please offer her a soda.
I am talking to you!

Pro Tip:
A subjective pronoun acts as the **subject** of the sentence.

Pro Tip:
An objective pronoun acts as the **object** of the sentence.

Let's Practice!

Instructions:
Circle the pronoun in each of the sentences below and indicate whether it is subjective or objective pronoun.

EXAMPLE:

Devin doesn't think that bacon is good for (me.)   _objective_

1.   It shouldn't be too long now.   _____

2.   Are they going to run a marathon?   _____

3.   Running a marathon would be hard for them.   _____

4.   Steven promised to give you an expensive gift.   _____

5.   Well, this certainly feels like an odd thing to say.   _____

Your turn!

Instructions:
Write sentences using the pronouns below. Circle the pronouns when you use them and write S for subjective and O for objective above the circles.

1.   you   _____

2.   he   _____

3.   him   _____

4.   I   _____

Intensive and Reflexive Pronouns

Intensive:

I built that cabinet **myself**.

Juliet **herself** is the only one people trust.

Reflexive:

I built **myself** that cabinet.

Juliet gave **herself** a birthday present.

Pro Tip:
An **intensive** pronoun emphasizes, or intensifies, a noun or another pronoun.

Pro Tip:
A **reflexive** pronoun directs the action of the verb back to the subject of the sentence.

Let's Practice!

Instructions:
In each of the following sentences, indicate whether <u>underlined pronoun</u> is intensive or reflexive and draw an arrow to its antecedent.

EXAMPLE:

We always treat **ourselves** to ice cream cones after rehearsal.   _____reflexive_____

1.   You should sing **yourself** your favorite song whenever you're sad.   _____

2.   Can you believe that we made that table **ourselves**?   _____

3.   That book was written by J.K. Rowling **herself**.   _____

4.   Every night at nine o'clock, the streetlight turns **itself** off.   _____

5.   Luis bought **himself** a box of chocolates yesterday.   _____

Your turn!

Instructions:
Write sentences using the pronouns below as indicated: (R) for reflexive and (I) for intensive. Circle each pronoun and draw an arrow to its antecedent.

1. herself (R)   _____

2. ourselves (I)   _____

3. itself (I)   _____

Grammaropolis

Pronoun or Adjective?

Adjective:
<u>This</u> car is one of the safest cars on the market today.

Pronoun:
<u>This</u> is one of the safest cars on the market today.

Pro Tip:
Some words can be either pronouns or adjectives, depending on how they're used in the sentence.

Let's Practice!

Instructions:
Indicate whether the <u>underlined word</u> is an adjective or a pronoun. If it is an adjective, draw an arrow to the word it modifies. If it is a pronoun, draw an arrow to its antecedent (the word it replaces).

EXAMPLE:

Susana wants me to give <u>her</u> a vanilla milkshake.   ____pronoun____

1.   <u>**Some**</u> people think that the chupacabras isn't real.   _____

2.   <u>**Those**</u> are not my dirty footprints.   _____

3.   Victoria invited us all over to <u>**her**</u> house for snacks.   _____

4.   <u>**This**</u> cat just knocked over my flower vase.   _____

5.   Lola passed me the mashed potatoes, but I didn't want <u>**any**</u>.   _____

Your turn!

Instructions:
Write sentences using the words below as indicated: (A) for adjective and (P) for pronoun. Don't forget to circle the word in each sentence.

1. that (A) _____

2. any (A) _____

3. some (P) _____

4. those (P)_____

Writing with Pronouns

INSTRUCTIONS (PART ONE):
Brainstorm four people and list their corresponding pronouns, and then brainstorm four things and list their corresponding pronouns. Remember that your pronouns can be subjective or objective!

	PERSON	PRONOUN		THING	PRONOUN
1.	Mr. Vaughn /	he	1.	grass /	it
2.	/		2.	/	
3.	/		3.	/	
4.	/		4.	/	
5.	/		5.	/	

INSTRUCTIONS (PART TWO):
Now write a story that incorporates at least two of the people and at least two of the things from your lists above. Remember to use both the pronouns **and** the antecedents! Circle the pronouns when you use them.

_____

_____

_____

_____

_____

_____

_____

The Big Pronoun Quiz!

INSTRUCTIONS: Identify the antecedent (the word the <u>underlined pronoun</u> replaces) from the options below.

1. A good leader knows that all the responsibility is ultimately <u>hers</u>.
   - ○ leader
   - ○ responsibility
   - ○ knows
   - ○ that

2. That silly cat covered <u>itself</u> in green paint when it leapt against the wall.
   - ○ That
   - ○ paint
   - ○ cat
   - ○ wall

3. My favorite thing about Charles is that <u>he</u> is so considerate.
   - ○ thing
   - ○ Charles
   - ○ favorite
   - ○ considerate

4. Erica and I asked our parents if they would give <u>us</u> some more dessert.
   - ○ Erica and I
   - ○ parents
   - ○ dessert
   - ○ Erica

5. I don't know who those shoes belong to, but they're definitely not <u>mine</u>.
   - ○ I
   - ○ those
   - ○ they're
   - ○ shoes

INSTRUCTIONS: Indicate whether the <u>underlined pronouns</u> below are reflexive or intensive.

6. Helena asked for help because she couldn't do it all <u>herself</u>.
   - ○ reflexive
   - ○ intensive

7. The sparrows clean <u>themselves</u> in the rain gutters along the rooftops.
   - ○ reflexive
   - ○ intensive

8. We taught <u>ourselves</u> how to bake cookies!
   - ○ reflexive
   - ○ intensive

9. I <u>myself</u> am the best choice to lead this company into the future.
   - ○ reflexive
   - ○ intensive

10. You should ask <u>yourself</u> if you really want to do this right now.
    - ○ reflexive
    - ○ intensive

Grammaropolis

Meet the Conjunctions!

EXAMPLES

JOINING WORDS: Savannah **and** Roxanne ate cookies **and** cake.

JOINING PHRASES: Did you find your keys on the table **or** in your pocket?

JOINING CLAUSES: I've never met Julian, **but** he seems nice.

Coordinating Conjunctions

Words
Should I wear shorts _or_ pants?

Phrases
Paige dove over the hedge _and_ onto her lawn.

Complete Thoughts
Rolo is my favorite cat, _for_ he always snuggles with me.

Pro Tip:
The FANBOYS (also known as coordinating conjunctions) are used to join **words**, **phrases**, or **complete thoughts** (independent clauses).

Let's practice!

Instructions:
Circle all of the coordinating conjunctions in the sentences below.

EXAMPLE:
The house was cold (and) dark, (but) we had to go inside anyway.

1. I don't watch movies, nor do I watch television.

2. My son says I type loudly, but he loves me anyway.

3. Many dogs and cats don't get along, yet mine seem to love each other.

4. Order the pickles or the onion rings, for both of those dishes are spectacular.

5. Henri's phone ran out of battery, so he had to borrow his sister's phone.

Your turn!

Instructions:
Write sentences using the following conjunctions to join words or word groups.
Don't forget to circle the conjunction in the sentence!

1. but _____

2. and _____

3. so _____

Correlative Conjunctions

I am **neither** happy **nor** sad right now.

Gavin **not only** plays the violin **but also** composes his own music.

Pro Tip:
A **correlative conjunction** is a two-part conjunction used to join words or phrases used in the same way.

Pro Tip:
Common correlative conjunctions are **either/or**, **neither/nor**, **whether/or**, and **not only/but also**.

Let's Practice!

Instructions:
Circle both parts of the correlative conjunction in each of the following sentences and draw a line linking the two parts.

EXAMPLE:
Neither my aunt Etta nor my cousin James came to my birthday party.

1.   Enrique has to go to school whether it rains or it snows.

2.   Both Jason and Mason play badminton.

3.   I think I will choose either the chocolate pudding or the vanilla cupcakes.

4.   Bella enjoys not only classical music but also punk rock.

5.   Neither Minecraft nor Roblox provides my favorite gaming experience.

Your turn!

Instructions:
Write complete sentences using the correlative conjunctions below. Don't forget to circle and link both parts!

1. either/or   _____

2. both/and   _____

3. neither/nor   _____

Subordinating Conjunctions

Subordinate Clause First

<u>Since</u> you don't like pickles, I took them off your sandwich.

<u>Now that</u> Felipe is here, we can start the meeting.

Subordinate Clause Second

I took the pickles off your sandwich <u>since</u> you don't like them.

We can start the meeting <u>now that</u> Felipe is here.

Pro Tip:
A **subordinating conjunction** introduces a subordinate, or dependent, clause.

Pro Tip:
The subordinate clause can come before or after the independent clause.

Let's Practice!

Instructions:
Circle the subordinating conjunction in each of the following sentences and then underline the entire subordinate clause.

EXAMPLE:

(Wherever) <u>you end up moving</u>, I hope you live near good restaurants.

1. Devon won't spend the night at our house unless we promise not to scare her.

2. Even though it's raining today, people still want to go to the zoo.

3. If Gbemi's computer works, she will be able to do all of her homework.

4. You only want to play soccer because you like wearing shinguards.

5. After Carlos finishes his dinner, he will ask for dessert.

Your turn!

Instructions:
Write complete sentences using each of the subordinating conjunctions below to introduce a subordinate clause. Don't forget to circle the conjunction and underline the entire subordinate clause!

1. now that _____

2. after _____

3. since _____

Identifying Conjunctions

Without Conjunctions:
Sam will buy apples at the store. He will buy sugar. He will buy cinnamon. He likes baking. He likes eating the food he bakes.

With Conjunctions:
Sam will buy apples, cinnamon, **and** sugar at the store **because** he **not only** likes baking **but also** likes eating the food he bakes.

Pro Tip:
Conjunctions make it possible to link words and ideas together in many different ways.

Let's Practice!

Instructions:
Circle all of the conjunctions in each of the following sentences.

EXAMPLE:
Juliet normally doesn't like fish (or) spinach, (yet) she ate everything on her plate!

1. Whenever I think of teddy bears, I want to laugh and sing.

2. Charles won't go to school because he has chills and a high fever.

3. Will you either give Manuel job or tell him to go home?

4. After they go to the movie, they will all go back to their own houses.

5. Unless you can control your dog, we'll have to run away and hide from it.

Your turn!

Instructions:
Write sentences that incorporate each of the words below as conjunctions. Don't forget to circle the conjunctions!

1. since _____

2. and _____

3. neither/nor _____

Writing with Conjunctions

Name:

INSTRUCTIONS (PART ONE):
Circle THREE coordinating conjunctions and TWO subordinating conjunctions from among the choices below.

COORDINATING

for
and
nor
but
or
yet
so

SUBORDINATING

after	even if	though
although	even though	unless
as	if	until
because	now that	whenever
before	once	wherever
by the time	since	while

INSTRUCTIONS (PART TWO):
Now write a story that incorporates the conjunctions you have circled. Remember to circle the conjunctions once you use them in the story as well!

_____

_____

_____

_____

_____

_____

_____

The Big Conjunction Quiz!

INSTRUCTIONS: Indicate the correct type of conjunction for each of the <u>underlined conjunctions</u> below.

1. Jason can often hear the birds outside his window, <u>but</u> he can never see them.
   ○ coordinating   ○ correlative   ○ subordinating

2. <u>Whenever</u> Farshan starts his day with prayer and meditation, he feels great.
   ○ coordinating   ○ correlative   ○ subordinating

3. <u>Though</u> they disagree about sports, Christina and Cynthia are friends.
   ○ coordinating   ○ correlative   ○ subordinating

4. Unfortunately, that project is on hold <u>until</u> more resources become available.
   ○ coordinating   ○ correlative   ○ subordinating

5. Anju kept her sari clean and pressed, <u>for</u> the Festival of Lights was approaching.
   ○ coordinating   ○ correlative   ○ subordinating

6. <u>Both</u> Puccini <u>and</u> Verdi were Italian opera composers.
   ○ coordinating   ○ correlative   ○ subordinating

7. Kristin's favorite color is purple, <u>and</u> her brother's favorite color is pink.
   ○ coordinating   ○ correlative   ○ subordinating

8. I'll give you two options for dinner: peas <u>or</u> carrots.
   ○ coordinating   ○ correlative   ○ subordinating

9. Jocelyn read the book <u>before</u> she saw the movie version.
   ○ coordinating   ○ correlative   ○ subordinating

10. The fans trudged out of the stadium, <u>for</u> the home team lost badly.
    ○ coordinating   ○ correlative   ○ subordinating

Grammaropolis

Meet the Prepositions!

I am a preposition!

I show the relationship between the object (a noun or pronoun) and other words in the sentence.

EXAMPLES

WHERE: I left my keys <u>under</u> the book <u>on</u> my desk.

WHEN: Sadie always reads <u>before</u> bedtime.

LOGICAL: Helena only eats blueberries <u>with</u> whipped cream.

Identifying Prepositions

Space (where)
Jake hit the ball <u>over</u> the fence.

Time (when)
Please come home <u>after</u> school.

Logical Relationship
Stella left <u>for</u> college yesterday.

Pro Tip:
A preposition locates an object in **time** or **space** or shows a **logical relationship** between the object and the rest of the sentence.

Pro Tip:
A preposition that is more than one word but acts as a single preposition is called a **compound preposition.** Examples include: **next to, instead of, because of,** and **due to.**

Let's practice!

Instructions:
Circle the prepositions in the following sentences and then indicate whether they help tell when or where the action of the verb happens or if they show a logical relationship. Don't forget to look for compound prepositions!

EXAMPLE:
School was canceled because of the snow.   __logical__

1. Please don't eat anything before lunch.   _____

2. Aaron came home with seventeen chocolate bars.   _____

3. I ran toward the tallest tree I could see.   _____

4. The class came together outside the main building.   _____

5. Do you ever eat raspberries in the winter?   _____

Your turn!

Instructions:
Finish the sentences below by incorporating your own prepositions. Don't forget to circle the prepositions!

1. <u>Dayton played his game</u> _____

2. <u>Molly and Reggie jumped</u> _____

3. <u>Nell's restaurant is closed</u> _____

Prepositional Phrases

A preposition is placed at the beginning of a prepositional phrase.

<u>**above**</u> my bed

<u>**throughout**</u> the month

Pro Tip:
A prepositional phrase starts with a preposition and ends with the object of the preposition.

Let's practice!

Instructions:
In each of the following sentences, underline the entire prepositional phrase and circle the preposition. There may be more than one!

EXAMPLE:
Wille left his drink next to his keyboard on the desk in his room.

1. We are definitely playing this game by the rules.

2. I leaned against the wall in Billy's backyard.

3. Giles hasn't seen his sister since Tuesday at noon.

4. At school yesterday, Xander tripped on the edge of the sidewalk.

5. They ran through the hallway toward the open door.

Your turn!

Instructions:
Write sentences that incorporate the prepositional phrases below. Remember to underline the prepositional phrases and circle the prepositions.

1. under the rug _____

2. like a cat _____

3. until Friday _____

Preposition or Adverb?

Adverb
Kyle fell <u>down</u>.
"down" is by itself, without the rest of a phrase. That means it's an adverb.

Preposition
Kyle fell <u>down the stairs</u>.
"down the stairs" is a prepositional phrase, so down is a preposition.

Pro Tip:
Some words can be used as either prepositions or adverbs. Remember that a preposition always has to be at the front of the phrase. If there's no phrase, it's not a preposition!

Let's Practice!

Instructions:
Indicate whether the <u>underlined word</u> is a preposition or an adverb. If it is a preposition, draw an arrow to the object of the phrase. If it is an adverb, draw an arrow to the word it modifies.

EXAMPLE:
When Delilah looked <u>**around**</u>, she saw that she wasn't alone. _____adverb_____

1. Delila looked <u>**around**</u> the classroom for something to do. _____

2. When it got dark last night, our parents called us <u>**inside**</u>. _____

3. Varian looked <u>**inside**</u> the box that his sister had given him. _____

4. By the time we arrived, the marathoners had already run <u>**by**</u>. _____

5. Dad ran <u>**by**</u> the house to pick up something he'd forgotten. _____

Your turn!

Instructions:
Write sentences using the words below as adverbs (A) or prepositions (P) as indicated. If it is a preposition, draw an arrow to the object of the phrase. If it is an adverb, draw an arrow to the word it modifies.

1. in (A) _____

2. in (P) _____

3. outside (P)_____

4. outside (A)_____

Writing with Prepositions

Name: _____

INSTRUCTIONS (PART ONE):

Create six prepositional phrases with the prepositions below.

above	behind	down	near	through
across	below	during	off	throughout
after	beneath	from	on	to
against	beside	in	out	toward
around	between	inside	outside	under
at	beyond	into	over	until
before	by		since	upon

1. _____

2. _____

3. _____

4. _____

5. _____

6. _____

INSTRUCTIONS (PART TWO):

Now write a story that incorporates the prepositions you have circled. Remember to circle the prepositions once you use them in the story as well!

_____

_____

_____

_____

_____

_____

Grammaropolis

The Big Preposition Quiz!

INSTRUCTIONS: Indicate whether the <u>underlined prepositions</u> below help tell where, when, or show a logical relationship.

1. I just received a vase filled <u>with</u> long-stemmed roses.

    ○ where   ○ when   ○ logical relationship

2. Thick green ivy climbed <u>up</u> the cemetery walls.

    ○ where   ○ when   ○ logical relationship

3. A newspaper cartoonist draws pictures <u>of</u> politicians and celebrities.

    ○ where   ○ when   ○ logical relationship

4. Gavin built his house <u>between</u> a large oak tree and a pear-shaped pond.

    ○ where   ○ when   ○ logical relationship

5. Wilson always goes to the ice cream shop with his friends <u>after</u> school.

    ○ where   ○ when   ○ logical relationship

INSTRUCTIONS: Indicate whether the <u>underlined words</u> below are prepositions or an adverbs.

6. The library door suddenly swung <u>open</u>, and the librarian appeared in the doorway.

    ○ preposition   ○ adverb

7. I really wish someone would <u>open</u> a window.

    ○ preposition   ○ adverb

8. Sometimes Frank just likes to sit by the river and watch the ducks swim <u>by</u>.

    ○ preposition   ○ adverb

9. Have you ever met Frank? He's the guy always sitting <u>by</u> the river.

    ○ preposition   ○ adverb

10. Those apples are still fresh enough to eat; please don't throw them <u>out</u>.

    ○ preposition   ○ adverb

Grammaropolis

Meet the Interjections!

EXAMPLES

MILD EMOTION: <u>Wow</u>, that is a really big bird.

STRONG EMOTION: <u>Eww</u>! I'm not going eat that!

Identifying Interjections

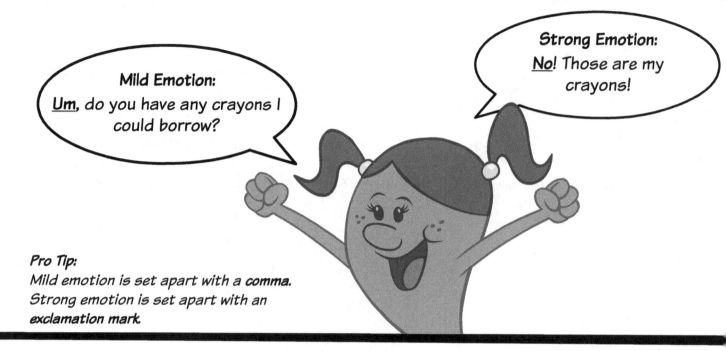

Mild Emotion:

<u>Um</u>, do you have any crayons I could borrow?

Strong Emotion:

<u>No</u>! Those are my crayons!

Pro Tip:

*Mild emotion is set apart with a **comma**.*
*Strong emotion is set apart with an **exclamation mark**.*

Let's practice!

Instructions:
Circle the interjection in each of the following sentences and indicate whether it is expressing mild or strong emotion.

EXAMPLE:

(Hey,) have you ever seen anything like this?   __mild__

1. "Ouch!" he exclaimed. "I just stubbed my toe!"   _____

2. Gee, that's a pretty cool flower.   _____

3. Yay! I just found a dollar.   _____

4. Drat! My favorite team just lost the big game.   _____

5. "Yum," Quinton said. "I do like sandwiches."   _____

Your turn!

Instructions:
Write sentences using the interjections below to express mild or strong emotion, as indicated.

1. Well (mild)   _____

2. Yeah (strong)   _____

3. Shh (strong)   _____

Writing with Interjections

INSTRUCTIONS (PART ONE):

Write down ten interjections you might use to express mild or strong emotion. Feel free to make up a few of them if you want! Circle your six favorite ones.

1._____   6._____

2._____   7._____

3._____   8._____

4._____   9._____

5._____   10._____

INSTRUCTIONS (PART TWO):

Now write sentences using your favorite interjections. Remember to use a comma when you express mild emotion and an exclamation mark with strong emotion!

MILD EMOTION

1. _____

2. _____

3. _____

STRONG EMOTION:

1. _____

2. _____

3. _____

The Big Interjection Quiz!

INSTRUCTIONS: Identify the interjection in each of the sentences below from among the available options.

1. Phew! That wind is strong enough to blow my house down.
    - ○ That
    - ○ strong
    - ○ Phew
    - ○ wind

2. Hey! You need to come over to this side of the street before you get hurt.
    - ○ Hey
    - ○ come
    - ○ You
    - ○ street

3. Hmmm, that sure is an interesting thing for you to say.
    - ○ sure
    - ○ that
    - ○ you
    - ○ Hmmm

4. "Yikes!" screamed my sister when she saw a mouse. "That's a mouse!"
    - ○ mouse
    - ○ screamed
    - ○ Yikes
    - ○ That's

5. I'm pretty sure that I answered all of Mrs. Felton's questions correctly. Yes!
    - ○ correctly
    - ○ Yes
    - ○ pretty
    - ○ sure

INSTRUCTIONS: Indicate whether the <u>underlined interjections</u> below express mild emotion or strong emotion.

6. <u>Yeah,</u> I really do respect my teachers.
    - ○ mild emotion
    - ○ strong emotion

7. <u>Aargh!</u> Mean-spirited people make me so angry!
    - ○ mild emotion
    - ○ strong emotion

8. <u>Hey,</u> have you ever heard of a band called The Dill Pickles?
    - ○ mild emotion
    - ○ strong emotion

9. <u>C'mon!</u> That was a foul!
    - ○ mild emotion
    - ○ strong emotion

10. <u>Aah,</u> there's nothing quite like the feeling of sunshine on my cheeks.
    - ○ mild emotion
    - ○ strong emotion

Grammaropolis

The Big Quiz Answer Key!

NOUNS

1. collective
2. compound
3. abstract
4. proper
5. collective
6. plural
7. singular
8. singular
9. plural
10. singular

PRONOUNS

1. responsibility
2. cat
3. Charles
4. Erica and I
5. shoes
6. intensive
7. reflexive
8. reflexive
9. intensive
10. reflexive

VERBS

1. linking verb
2. action verb
3. action verb
4. linking verb
5. action verb
6. transitive
7. intransitive
8. transitive
9. transitive
10. intransitive

CONJUNCTIONS

1. coordinating
2. subordinating
3. subordinating
4. subordinating
5. coordinating
6. correlative
7. coordinating
8. coordinating
9. subordinating
10. coordinating

ADJECTIVES

1. what kind
2. which one
3. how much
4. how many
5. what kind
6. respect
7. earth
8. tent
9. weeds
10. people

PREPOSITIONS

1. logical
2. where
3. logical
4. where
5. when
6. adverb
7. preposition
8. adverb
9. preposition
10. adverb

ADVERBS

1. often
2. forth
3. wistfully
4. never
5. home
6. when
7. when
8. where
9. how
10. how

INTERJECTIONS

1. Phew
2. Hey
3. Hmm
4. Yikes
5. Yes
6. mild
7. strong
8. mild
9. strong
10. mild

- ☑ Innovative and engaging
- ☑ Aligned to state standards
- ☑ Addresses various learning styles
- ☑ Created and refined in the ultimate proving grounds: the classroom

THE STORYBOOKS

4/24/2019 | $6.99
Paperback | 32 pages | 8" x 8"
Full-color illustrations throughout
Includes instructional back matter
Ages 7 to 11 | Grades 1 to 5
JUVENILE NONFICTION /
LANGUAGE ARTS / GRAMMAR

9781644420157 | Noun
9781644420171 | Verb
9781644420133 | Adjective
9781644420102 | Adverb
9781644420164 | Pronoun
9781644420119 | Conjunction
9781644420140 | Preposition
9781644420126 | Interjection

- An eight-book series starring the parts of speech, which are personified based on the roles they play in the sentence.

- Featuring a different character-based adventure for every part of speech.

- Each book includes standards–aligned definitions and examples, just like you'd find in a textbook (but way more fun).

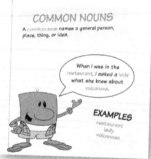

THE WORKBOOKS

3/03/2020 | $12.99 | B&W
PB | 64 pages | 11"H x 8.5"W
Includes quizzes & instruction
Ages 7 to 11 | Grades 1 to 5
JUVENILE NONFICTION /
LANGUAGE ARTS / GRAMMAR

9781644420300 | Grade 1
9781644420317 | Grade 2
9781644420324 | Grade 3
9781644420331 | Grade 4
9781644420188 | Grade 5

- Skill-building workbooks featuring character-based instruction along with various comprehension checks and writing exercises.

- Aligned to Common Core and state standards for K–5.

Grammaropolis is available through Ingram Publisher Services.
Contact your IPS Sales Representative to order.
Call (866) 400-5351, Fax (800) 838-1149, ips@ingramcontent.com, or visit ipage.

CPSIA information can be obtained
at www.ICGtesting.com
Printed in the USA
JSHW011439291020
9117JS00002B/4

9 781644 420324